T0128201

THE MILLIPEDE EFFECT

My Quest to Understand and Help
the Homeless, Stranded and Down and Out

RODNEY D. BROOKS

President and Founder,
Brothers Brooks Vision 2 Mission LLC

authorHOUSE®

AuthorHouse™
1663 Liberty Drive
Bloomington, IN 47403
www.authorhouse.com
Phone: 1 (800) 839-8640

Published by AuthorHouse   01/24/2017

ISBN: 978-1-5246-5777-2 (sc)
ISBN: 978-1-5246-5775-8 (hc)
ISBN: 978-1-5246-5776-5 (e)

Library of Congress Control Number: 2016921588

Print information available on the last page.

Contents

Acknowledgments

Working with the homeless, the stranded, and the down and out has encouraged me to search the depths of my soul for understanding. I give a special thank you to the many agencies, foundations, civic organizations, and volunteers who, on a daily basis, make it their purpose and mission to meet the needs of those who are less fortunate and vulnerable. I have a new level of appreciation for the countless who make it their cause to fight, serve, and educate about this great cause. I salute you!

To my family members—Nancy, Rhonda, Rodney Jr., Ben, and Breanne Brooks and Jaliyah Taylor—I appreciate your support of me during the writing of this book and your efforts to support the homeless as well. As you handed out care packages and fed the homeless, stranded, and down and out, I believe our family gained a deeper appreciation of this mission and God's purpose for us—to serve as he has instructed us.

To Fannie Johnson, executive director of L.O.V.E.'s Kitchen, who continues to feed and take care of the homeless in a way that can only be compared to a mother who is taking care of her children. You will be blessed as you are a living embodiment of the scripture.

I thank the following individuals whose words through scripture and sermons have inspired and guided me: Dr. Robert Cain, Rev. Jimmy

Johnson, Dr. Erwin Lutzer, Dr. Tony Evans, Dr. David Jeremiah, Rev. Chuck Swindoll, and Dr. Jack Graham.

Special and number one thanks go to God and my Lord and Savior Jesus Christ, who has allowed me to be used as a vessel in his efforts to support those who are homeless, stranded, and down and out. All praises go to God!

CHAPTER 1

The Millipede

The millipede is a myriapod invertebrate with an elongated body composed of many segments, most of which bear two pairs of legs. Each of these segments is actually two segments fused together as one. The word millipede is formed from the Latin word for 1,000, but there is no evidence that millipedes have a thousand legs. The millipede's body is similar to a long train in that it has a series of connected sections. However, a train has railcars with wheels, and each section does not have the ability to work independently of the others. The millipede's first segment and usually its last segment have single pairs of legs while the other segments are double-legged. All the segments work in collaboration with each other. The millipede grows as it ages by adding segments to the body and legs to each segment.

Millipedes are among the oldest known animals. They are hunted and preyed upon by various animals, including reptiles, birds, mammals, and insects. Other invertebrates have specialized structures that allow them to feed on millipedes.

The millipede moves slowly; all of its legs work together and in sync. On one side, each pair of legs moves together in the same direction and in the opposite direction on the other side, creating a rippling effect.

Rodney D. Brooks

Most millipedes are detritivores, i.e., they feed on decomposing vegetation, feces, and organic matter mixed with soil. They often play important roles in the breakdown and decomposition of leaf litter, which is fragmented in the millipede's gut and excreted as pellets on leaf fragments, algae, fungi, and bacteria that facilitate the decomposition by the microorganisms (1). Some millipedes are herbivorous and feed on living plants, and some species can become serious pests to crops.

CHAPTER 2

My Thoughts

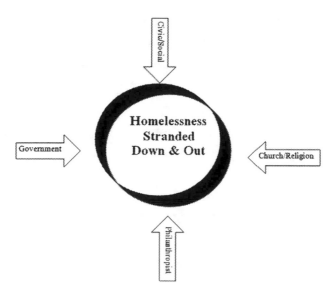

When you think about someone who is homeless, stranded, or down and out, I am sure all kinds of things come to mind. Some are real and some are perceived, but all determine how you will act toward that individual or someone in that situation.

My interest in the matter is not something that is a mountain-top revelation; nor does it make my effort any greater than the next person's. What you will find in this book is my effort to do my part in this century-long struggle and hopefully a common person's perspective (i.e., not the view of a government, organized religion, or social organization, although each group plays a huge part in tackling this problem). Through my faith and belief, I want to find ways to tackle this problem.

There are a great many obstacles facing us in this fight to help those in need. Many great people are doing their part; however, the issues are still here, and on some fronts, they are getting worse. Many individuals are working tirelessly to address a host of concerns. If I could give all of them kudos, I would. Many people are on a mission to deal with the major problems this country faces regarding the homeless. If only one person tried, it would be a monumental task. It will take a collective effort—individuals in conjunction with the government, religious organizations, and social organizations.

Just how big is the homeless population? The numbers have ranged from 3 million to 3.5 million in any given year, which is roughly 1 percent of the US population.

Keep Your Coins

I Want
Change

CHAPTER 3
What Is Homelessness?

Ask most people what homelessness is, and you may hear "someone who is out on the street, sleeping under a bridge, and begging for help."

Ask those same individuals what circumstances may have caused an individual to become homeless, and the answers will vary widely based upon people's experiences. Most of our understanding and interpretations are based on our perceptions, what we hear from others, and even movies and other entertainment. Sometimes our idea of a homeless person is based on how we look at ourselves.

The Pursuit of Happyness

By now many people have read, or at least heard about, Chris Gardner's autobiography, which described his one-year struggle with homelessness after facing a series of unfortunate challenges. The movie *The Pursuit of Happyness* starred Hollywood acting sensation Will Smith as Chris Gardner and shined a light on how a hardworking individual with motivation and initiative can end up homeless. If watching the movie was your first understanding of the problem, you might believe that with the right will and determination anyone should be able to beat the saga of homelessness. The Chris Gardner story is remarkable, one that should be admired by all.

The PURSUIT OF HAPPYNESS

Billy Ray Valentine Versus Louis Winthorpe III

In 1983, an interesting comedy movie directed by John Landis hit theaters. *Trading Places* starred some of the biggest actors in the movie industry—Eddie Murphy, Dan Aykroyd, Ralph Bellamy, Don Ameche, and Jamie Lee Curtis—and was one of the highest-grossing films of the year. The story centered on a bet made by the Duke brothers (Bellamy and Ameche) that involved making two individuals from different social settings trade places to see if environment or upbringing (nature versus nurture) is the cause of success or failure. Billy Ray Valentine (Eddie Murphy) is a homeless street hustler who pretends to be a disabled veteran and Louis Winthorpe III (Dan Aykroyd) is an educated commodities broker. The movie provided two major reasons a person can become homeless and some ideas about what a person will do once that occurs.

At one point, Billy Ray is asked why he is homeless and why he turned to a life of crime. He is asked whether he had come from a broken home and had ever been shown love, among other similar questions. How we view those who are homeless, stranded, or down and out depends on our perspective and the mental models that we form throughout our lives.

Those models not only give us mental perceptions, they also trigger our actions toward the homeless, stranded, and down and out.

TRADING PLACES

Gang Related

The plot of the 1997 movie *Gang Related* centers around a couple of corrupt DEA agents, played by James Belushi and Tupac Shakur, who end up killing a narcotics dealer illegally and then blaming the killing on a homeless individual named Joe Doe (Dennis Quaid). The agents blame the killing on someone who is homeless because he fits the stereotype of a potential criminal.

The plot continues all the way until the court date, and it appears the case is a slam dunk for the two agents. But the real identity of Joe Doe is determined by his lawyer, played by James Earl Jones, who reveals that Joe Doe is really William McCall—heir to a financial institution and a noted surgeon who had tended to the poor and had been presumed dead. In the end, all works out for Joe Doe/William McCall. But how many other homeless people have been wrongly accused or stereotyped in a manner that has left them without certain services or opportunities?

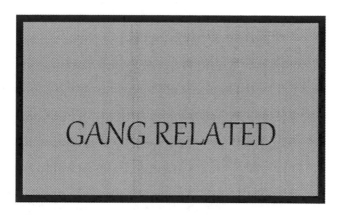

GANG RELATED

Common Perceptions About the Homeless

There are a number of perceptions regarding why some people are homeless, including:

- They are criminals.
- They are con artists.
- They are lazy and don't want to work.
- They are drug addicts and winos.
- They are mentally ill.
- They are disabled.

One individual's perception often becomes another person's reality. Although I call them perceptions, in each of them, there is an element of truth that can be found in all parts of society. It is not a homeless issue but a societal issue. Let's take a look at each of these perceptions a little bit further.

They Are Criminals

It is safe to say a good number of individuals who are released from jail may end up homeless. If you have no family support structure, then where will you go when you are released? If you now have a felony record, how do you find suitable employment? If you have no money, how do you eat or find suitable housing? If you have been incarcerated for some time, then all of your belongings are no longer available. Your credit history will be nonexistent.

All of these things can hamper a person trying to get a fresh start. These factors can make it difficult to function in society without being dependent upon someone else. Such a situation could easily push some back to a life of crime just to survive. The choice between engaging in criminal activity and possibly getting caught becomes a viable option for some faced with the harsh reality of sleeping on asphalt or sleeping under a bridge in extreme elements—whether it is 28 degrees or 102 degrees—lying in the rain or snow without any shelter, going without medicine if you are sick, and not knowing from where your next meal will come. For some, even jail sounds more appealing.

Now to those who perceive that all homeless individuals are criminals and that their criminal activity is contagious and can be caught by those who try to help, all I can say is maybe or maybe not. Criminal behavior also occurs among people who are not homeless. I can say without a shadow of a doubt that not all homeless people are criminals.

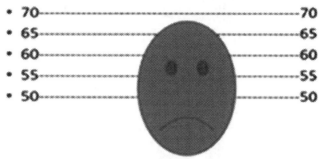

Mug Shot

They Are Con Artists

Every one of us can think about a time when we witnessed someone standing on the corner of a busy intersection, under an overpass, or outside of a store soliciting aid. We may have wondered if that individual was legitimate. We have seen healthy-looking individuals holding signs that read "homeless," and we probably thought, *That individual needs to get a job* or *where did he get the pen and cardboard to make that sign?*

How about the person you've seen on the corner on several occasions? Have you wondered if he was being honest? You have probably said to yourself, *Now this is ridiculous; he has been here doing the same thing over and over.* The thought is that they are not homeless but running a scam. There are stories of individuals who hold signs seeking assistance and are later seen driving off in nice vehicles? Is it feasible to follow someone around after you have assisted them? Movies depict individuals who pretend to be homeless, and then change into another set of clothes and go on with their normal lives. A gentleman where I live has been on various corners for more than nine months. One week I noticed him playing guitar and screaming at the vehicles as they passed by. I have personally talked with him and assisted him on numerous occasions.

Others might assume he is running some type of con. There may be some con artists who pretend to be homeless, down and out, or stranded. However, I believe that most of these individuals are not looking to run a con.

They Are Lazy and Don't Want to Work

At a time when people are being squeezed through taxes at all levels and government spending is out of control, working Americans are in a foul mood. If there is a hint of someone not working or contributing their fair share, it becomes a problem. America is a nation that was built upon the backs of the working class. Most Americans have no problem supporting those in need; however, the standard is if you don't work, then you don't eat. If you can work and are not working, then you are considered a dead beat. Now this thought process is given to us at an early age; it is as common as barbecue and apple pie in America. Our senses are high when it comes to the thought of someone freeloading or not wanting to work. Most of the time, when we see someone who is homeless and asking for money or assistance, our mental model process kicks in. We assess to see if that person is disabled, a child, or elderly. If they do not fall within those categories, then we ask, *Why can't they take care of themselves?* This assessment lasts about the amount of time it takes to take a quick glimpse in your side mirror and back onto the road. A quick read of the sign they are holding, a glance at their physicality and demeanor, and our minds are made up.

Some conclude that the person must be lazy, just wants a handout, and needs to go out and look for a job. Your senses are taken to a higher level if you see that person on more than one occasion. Your perception of this person rises even higher if you see the individual doing one of the following things: smoking, laughing, sitting or standing with others who are homeless and have the same physicality, or using a cell phone. Or perhaps he refuses to allow you to buy him a meal but would rather take the cash. Think about this: a homeless person has the ability to collect (on the low end) $15 a day or (on the high end) $100 a day by standing on the corner holding a sign stating "I am homeless and need help." At the same time, that same person could be living at a homeless shelter and eating at a food kitchen. What is the incentive to work? If the person does this for five days a week, he might collect between $65 and $500 per week tax free. What is the incentive for wanting to work? This scenario gives you the perception that this is a lazy individual or a con-artist. It is possible that some individuals who are homeless, down and out, or stranded are lazy, but that is not true about all of them.

Such thoughts may make one say, "I am not going to help any homeless individual." However that is like saying that all CEOs, COOs, and CFOs of major companies operate like the leaders of Enron did in the 1990s. However, to paint everyone with such a broad bush is unfair and the premise behind that belief is unfounded.

They Are Drug Addicts and Winos

Now this is an interesting one. How often has it crossed your mind that a homeless individual will take your money and purchase an alcoholic beverage? How often have you heard that a person lost everything due to a drug addiction and is now out on the street? One has to believe that there is some validity in these stories. Imagine an individual who is holding a sign that reads "homeless and hungry." You reach into your pocket and give him $2. You drive back later and see the individual coming out of a liquor store. That may change your mind about how you view the next person who holds a sign that reads "homeless and hungry."

Most people will do one of the following:

1) refuse to help the next homeless person they see;
2) offer to buy the person something to eat rather than give him money;
3) willingly help every homeless person with whom they come in contact, and chalk the previous experience up as an aberration.

Imagine several individuals standing in an open field around a fire in a trash can. They warm themselves next to the fire and pass around a liquor bottle. It sounds like a movie. This is another strong image we have of the homeless and their need for alcohol. We add to that image by believing that those individuals are unemployed and seek money only to quench their alcoholic thirst. Who can forget the images from various documentaries on drug addiction in the United States, in which several individuals talk about how their yearning for drugs caused them to lose everything, including their homes. You may not have heard them say they were drug free, so you wonder if these people will become criminals and steal or beg from others, like you, to get a couple of dollars for that next fix. Do you want your hard-earned money to enable someone else's alcohol or drug problem? I am pretty sure that there is some validity to the above scenarios, and there is probably some solid data out there with convincing numbers to reinforce these perceptions. There are probably several homeless individuals who are alcoholics and recovering alcoholics, caught up in a cycle of recovery and relapse.

I am reminded of a story told to me by a homeless gentleman I met in Mississippi. He calls himself Captain. He told me about one of his buddies, who was in the hospital, and how he had been warning him to leave that "junk" alone. Captain said his buddy collected money on the street to buy drugs. Captain said, "I told him that he was going to die soon." He added that he himself had been using drugs regularly several months earlier, until one day he was leaving a store, and he fainted and was taken to the hospital. He used to weigh 216 pounds, but upon his release from the hospital, he weighed only 147 pounds. While he was in the hospital he dreamed about two big doors. They were closed, and he tried to open them but he could not. A voice told him that he could not go in unless he got his life together. Captain said, "I believe that voice was God, and he was telling me that I was not going to heaven unless I got off those drugs. I try to warn my buddies to leave that junk alone." Although Captain's story could be considered a confirmation to those who link the homeless to drugs or alcohol, I would say that it is not a fair representation of all individuals who are homeless, stranded, or down and out. To believe all homeless are alcoholics or drug addicts could have an impact on those who are not and who may truly need a helping hand.

They Are Mentally Ill

We have all seen individuals walking or standing on the corner and thought to ourselves, *Something is strange about that individual.* Maybe it was a certain look, or he was acting in a way that seemed extremely odd. Perhaps they were talking to themselves. It is one of those images— once you see it you can't get it out of your mind. It is haunting and frightening to think that someone as vulnerable as a young child in the wilderness could be on the side of a road, living under a bridge, or wandering in a park, subject to all sorts of danger. A homeless person with a severe mental illness can be preyed upon in a way that can be cold and callous. However, there is another reaction we may have when we see those who are homeless and seem to have a mental illness—not pity, but fear.

This is the image of someone who may not have all of his faculties preying on others with a reckless abandon and no regard for the law or the rights of others. Such a frightening image tells you to get far away from that person quickly—to cross the street or hurry by this individual as soon as you can.

In the 1980s, I was working for a 7-11 convenience store in Little Rock, Arkansas. An older African American gentleman named Charlie would come through the area and just cause havoc. Charlie had a cane and his clothes were dirty. As he walked slowly with the cane, he would let out a stream of profanity. If anyone went close to him, he would swing that cane and curse out loud. Everyone called him Crazy Charlie. He would dig through trash cans and pick up old cigarette butts outside the store.

One day in June, I was listening to Charlie direct one of his tirades at some of kids outside, and I heard him say something that struck me as very odd. He said, "And you bastards do not even know the true meaning of Juneteenth." Juneteenth, also known as Juneteenth Independence Day or Freedom Day, is a holiday that commemorates the announcement of the abolition of slavery in Texas in June 1865. Once I heard Charlie say this, I realized the man was not crazy. I later struck up a conversation with him, and we became pretty good friends. I bought him food in the store and on occasion walked to his residence, which was an abandoned garage. It did not have any lights, only a dirty mattress and his belongings.

One night, I got a call from one of my coworkers, who said, "Rodney, Charlie is down here acting crazy and asking for you." I went to the store and asked Charlie what was going on.

He said, "I am hungry."

I can laugh about it now, but at the time I told Charlie, "Man, you can't come to the store behaving like that."

He replied, "Okay, Rodney."

There is no doubt that there are a considerable number of homeless individuals who have some type of mental illness and there is some truth to both images of one of meekness and one of fear. However, I don't believe every homeless person with a mental illness wants to do harm to others, and I would say there is very strong possibility that if these individuals could change their situation, they would.

They Are Disabled

This is one perception that may be a reality. Go to any large city where homeless people gather, and you will see several with disabilities, which can come in different forms—from the physical to mental (see previous discussion on mental illness). A disability is a physical or mental condition that limits a person's movement, senses, or activities and usually affects walking, talking, breathing, speaking, hearing, reasoning, and thinking. A good number of homeless individuals may have impairments that affect one of these areas. Disabled veterans are typically designated in a separate group. As a country, we believe we should care for those who sacrificed themselves for their country and were injured through no fault of their own. Occasionally, but not always, we can identify disabled veterans who are homeless.

The cynic in all of us sometimes wonders if certain individuals are telling us the truth about their disability status. Some con artists, like Billy Ray Valentine in *Trading Places*, validate our cynicism. It's easy to spot some physical disabilities, although we may not know if they occurred while on military duty or for some other reason. However, it is difficult to spot someone who is deaf unless you try talking to him; the same applies to someone who cannot speak. Since there are several reasons a person might be disabled, and not all of them are visible, it does not make much sense to assume that homeless people are lying about their physical abilities. There are various reasons a person could have a disability, including being sick or in an accident. I met a gentleman in a wheelchair who was homeless in Meridian, Mississippi, and his story was quite interesting. I noticed him sitting behind a convenience store around 4:30 p.m. on a Sunday afternoon. The temperature was around ninety-three degrees. I approached him and offered him one of my care packages, which I typically hand out to those who are homeless, stranded, or down and out. He took my package and then we spoke for about twenty-five minutes on how he'd lost one of his legs and how he tried to share his message with the youth in the area. He said they didn't listen to him and instead tried to steal from him, but that is another story.

He loved having fun, and that included drinking, smoking marijuana, and going to clubs. He did not care about much; just having fun was his thing. He did not listen to those who told him to slow down. He used to be a painter and described the art of painting a room in a house without using tape or a drop cloth. He stated that his skills were just that good. He spoke with pride when he described his artistic abilities. One night after getting drunk and high on marijuana, he got into an argument with a couple of guys and that the next thing he knew he was lying on the railroad tracks. He was so intoxicated that he could not get off the tracks, and a train severed his leg. He now sat in a wheelchair and could not walk (one leg was severed and the other did not function), wishing things were different. His painting days were over and he believed he'd just wasted his talent. Although he did have a place to stay, he considered himself down and out, with very little funds and dependent on others' financial generosity. Throughout our conversation, he quoted many biblical scriptures to help me to understand where he had been and where he was going. I can't speak to the validity of his story, but he was disabled. I am sure he could have gotten a piece of cardboard and made a sign that read "disabled veteran." But he did not, and it is for that reason I tell his story.

There are probably several individuals who are homeless and disabled, but everyone who is disabled is not homeless.

Some Actual Reasons Individuals Become Homeless

As noted earlier, the perceptions some have about the homeless are rooted in actual truth. However, there are other reasons that are equally compelling and hard to argue against; very few dispute these reasons, which include:

- Economics
    - Rising unemployment
    - Rising health-care costs
- Housing (bad mortgages)
- Natural disasters (and manmade disasters, such as house fires)
- Lack of funding at the local, state, and federal levels
- Domestic violence

Let's look at each of these in detail. Most people can get their minds around this list in sort of a positive way but the real challenge is when we see someone who is homeless. Do we rely on the first list—i.e., Common Perceptions About the Homeless—or this one?

Economics

I use the following generic description for economics: the method society uses to determine the production, distribution, and consumption of goods and services. Usually in a free-market society, those who produce are compensated for their production, which allows them to consume goods or services by paying others for what they have produced. Those goods or services may be food, housing, utilities, automobiles, health care, laundry services, clothes, airfare, haircuts, beds, aspirin, razors, lotion, and lawn care. Some of these things are essential and some are luxuries. However, without the means to purchase such goods or services, you can be left out of the economic process, at least legally.

Rising Unemployment

The unemployment rate in the United States is increasingly a political topic, but it is not my goal to speak about it on those terms. Although a 0-percent unemployment rate would be utopia, most people would say that anything under 6 percent would be ideal. Of course, a lot of factors would go into that. Stop and think about that number. It means that 6 percent of people willing and able to work will be unemployed. For every 100,000 people eligible to work, 6,000 would be unemployed. A 5.3-percent unemployment rate is equal to 8.3 million unemployed people. It is not hard to imagine that a significant portion of unemployed people may be homeless. Unfortunately, most homeless individuals are not accounted for in these statistics. Mergers and acquisitions, bank failures, plant closings, and business bankruptcies all have been devastating on the economy and have wiped out jobs and left millions unemployed and out on the streets. In a free-market economy, it is part of the economic process; however, there are real consequences for those who are left without.

I heard this story in a diversity workshop I attended. A group of bank employees had attended an earlier session of the workshop. The instructor was discussing stereotypes, and he noticed that the manager of the group, the VP, was observing his department during the discussion. The topic was how individuals feel when they meet someone homeless. The group had a very lively discussion, and the manager finally chimed in. The manager said that all homeless people are not who they seem to be. He had originally lived in the South and had moved to the East Coast with his family for a promising job opportunity. Things went well, and then suddenly the business folded, and he was without a job for quite a while. His wife got angry and left, as he could not find a job and could not make ends meet. He eventually ended up homeless. The manager said that his homeless travels led him to the street in front of the bank. He asked for money and food just like the other homeless individuals who were on the street, and just like the others, he was shunned and treated as despicable. He added that some of those individuals who passed him by were sitting in that workshop.

One day, while he was in front of the building, his current boss offered him a job as a janitor, and he accepted it. He told his boss about his background and his plight, about how he'd ended up on the street. His boss asked for his résumé, and the rest was history. Our instructor said that the eyes of people in that training class watered, and they had heavy hearts, feeling guilty or shameful about themselves. The manager said that he did not tell the story to make them feel bad but to help them understand that being homeless can happen to anyone. His issue was the economy, and he'd never thought it would happen to him. Our economic situation in the United States has made some people homeless, and there is no disputing that fact.

Rising Health-care Costs

I lost my job, which meant I lost my health-care coverage, and the cost was astronomical. I was offered COBRA benefits—extension of health benefits offered to those who lose their insurance coverage for reasons outlined under the Consolidated Omnibus Budget Reconciliation Act— and the cost was the total premium plus a 2-percent administrative cost. Luckily for me, my wife had coverage through her employer, and I did not have to use COBRA. Imagine losing your job and your income, and instead of roughly paying 20 percent of the cost of your insurance premium, you now have to pay 102 percent. We tell athletes that they are all just one injury away from not playing. The same can be said about most individuals; we are all just one major health issue—our own or that of a family member—from having our lives turned upside down, losing everything, and ending up on the street.

Housing

Of course, one would conclude that a person who is homeless would not have a place to live. What I refer to here, however, is that the lack of affordable housing or the cutback in affordable housing programs has contributed to the total number of homeless people in America. Triggered by unemployment, and stagnant wages, individuals have struggled over the years to find and keep a residence. The total number of bankruptcies due to the housing bubble of the 2000s as well as the slowdown in the home-building industries and the credit market hurt our entire economy and put many people out of work and individuals out of their homes. Now there are many different reasons for the housing bust, ranging from homeowner speculation to high-risk mortgage loans to questionable lending practices to the subprime mortgage market. It is hard to argue with Fannie Mae and Freddie Mac's mission to find ways to provide affordable housing for all. I leave the debate over the true reason for the bubble bust to the economists and pundits; however, individuals did end up homeless and thrust into the streets. Some people may believe that the individuals who became homeless were living beyond their means or were greedy; however, that was not always the case. Wanting to live the American dream is not a bad thing.

Natural Disasters

Who can forget the images of people at the Superdome during Hurricane Katrina or the more recent flooding in Florida, Louisiana, North Carolina, and South Carolina, or the thousands that were displaced due to other natural disasters? I went to New Orleans several years later and there were still several properties with an X on the roof to signify that the property was condemned. That is only one disaster, but there are many that do not get the headlines. Flooding, wildfires, earthquakes—are all a constant reminder of the devastation that Mother Nature causes. The most common disaster is the slew of tornadoes that go through the Midwest and the South like clockwork each year. Each of these disasters changed the landscape and people's lives. Natural disasters can have a double effect. The key places that are set up to help the homeless can be overwhelmed due to increasing numbers of people and those establishments themselves may be destroyed or damaged by wind, fire, floods, or rain. Agencies and organizations that help the homeless also have been getting squeezed due to the economic downturn; when a disaster hits, they frequently are tested beyond their limits. One of the most important things a state can hear during a disaster is that a disaster area has been declared, which means additional funding at the federal level will be granted. In 2009 President Obama signed the Homeless Emergency Assistance and Rapid Transition to Housing Act. Known as the Hearth Act, it amended the McKinley-Vento Homeless Assistance

Act, which clarified the definition of homelessness and sped up the process for local and state agencies to apply for and obtain funds from the federal government (2).

Lack of Funding at the Local, State, and Federal Levels

Funding for all government programs are down across the board, at every level. Some may say that it is due to tax policy; others will say that there is nothing to stimulate economic growth. Still others will say that the economy is not generating enough of the high-income jobs that will put a greater number of dollars into the treasury. Most economists agree that all these reasons are valid, and that there are plenty of others as well. These challenges have caused the federal, state and local governments to cut and slash their budgets, and this has ended the days of running up massive debt at the state and local levels. Two major areas that have been challenged by these cuts are social programs and education. With the rise in the costs of Social Security, Medicare and Medicaid, other social programs have been squeezed. There are only so many dollars that can be spread around without affecting defense (at the federal level) or security (at the federal, state, and local levels). That means the following programs must fight for dollars: food, housing, energy and utilities, education, training, services, child care and development, and community-development programs. At the federal level, most of these funds are given in block grants to the states, which then disburse them at the local level. Cuts at the federal level have a domino effect; dollars lost at the state and local levels must be made up by reducing funds somewhere else or decreasing programs and services. I will talk about the role of government in a later chapter. One of the things we always say in business is there is no such a thing as a write-off or deficit. At some point, you either must come up with the money to fund the program, or cut the program so you do not have to fund it.

Domestic Violence

Domestic violence is the emotional and/or physical control of an intimate partner and often involves tactics such as stalking and physical and sexual assaults. (3) When a woman decides to leave an abusive relationship, she often has nowhere to go. Many homeless women have experienced domestic violence in their adult lives. Most of the time these women have children, which can compound the problem if they are trying to get into a shelter. In my short experience, I have come across a few women who were homeless and trying to get away from an abusive relationship. These were among the few times in my journey that I felt helpless. It can be a dangerous situation. Just the topic of domestic violence causes people to say, "That situation is none of my business. Good intentions can go wrong very quickly." How many times have we seen women on the street and asked ourselves, *Why in the world is she out here?* or thought, *That situation does not look right.* But we pass them by, because those thoughts encourage us to avoid getting involved.

Domestic

Violence

CHAPTER 4

Awareness

You know that feeling when you buy a new car and you feel very special because you believe that new car is unique? Then, all of a sudden, you look around and see other cars just like yours. None of us are naive enough to believe that our new car is the only car the automotive company made. Our sense of recognition or awareness has been heightened, and we become more aware of other cars like the one that we have. Each day things go on around us that we barely notice.

A good example of this came from my former pastor. I am a deacon at St. John Missionary Baptist Church in Meridian, and our pastor, Reverend Johnson, would say: "Guys, there are a lot of people who are hurting right here in this neighborhood. Every day homeless individuals and prostitutes are walking right in our midst, and we are failing to meet their needs."

It wasn't until Pastor Johnson made those statements that I actually became aware of who was actually walking up and down the streets next to the church. Nothing changed; I became more informed and began to notice who was on the street. I became aware! I will address the role of the church a little later in the book.

I had always thought I could recognize the homeless. They were the ones standing at the intersection asking for money. At least that is what I thought. My pastor's comments aroused my awareness around the church but not beyond that. One day I was driving from Birmingham, AL, to Lorman, Mississippi, to pick up my son from college, and I had this thought of creating a business and leaving it for my kids. About two hours into the drive, I realized what I wanted to do in this business. I could not come up with an idea for a product. But I had learned quite a few things in my thirty-plus years of employment in various Fortune 100 and 500 companies, and I knew I could help others. The idea of helping the homelessness idea came to my head through various scriptures.

Around the third hour of my drive, I pulled off at an intersection in Jackson, Mississippi. I drove by the bus station, where I saw individuals from various walks of life. They were not holding signs but were lying on benches or just walking up and down the street. They had a peculiar look that I really had not noticed before, but my awareness meter had

Backpack

In Texas I noticed a considerable number of homeless individuals walking around with backpacks. Several of them told me that it allows them to be mobile and to protect their belongings.

Multiple Layers of Clothing on a Hot Day

The homeless individual cannot afford to leave his or her belongings in an unsecured place. To do so would invite someone to take those belongings. But on very hot days extra clothing can jeopardize one's health due to the extra heat that is captured on the body.

Dumpster/Garbage Cans

I have found individuals roaming around and rustling through dumpsters in search of food or clothes. On occasion when I went to offer assistance, the people rummaging let me know they were looking for cans, but they did appreciate that I cared. While in Houston I saw a gentleman walking through the neighborhood opening each garbage can to see what he could find. He told me he had lost his job, and he was trying to find whatever he could in the garbage. I gave him one of my care bags and departed. That was a pretty nice neighborhood. On one street alone I counted more than twenty-five garbage cans at different homes. I am familiar with the saying "one man's trash is another man's treasure," but that was sad to me.

Abandoned House

Individuals hang around abandoned houses, trying to find shelter and comfort. I have noticed this occurring when it grows close to dusk or night. There is definitely a difference between an abandoned house and a crack house.

The Bridge

Large bridges and overpasses provide shelter and protection from the elements and allow the homeless to be secluded from others.

Bus Stations

Anytime I go to a town I look for homeless, stranded, and down-and out individuals in bus stations. Some people are just trying to get ba home or somewhere other than where they are. Bus stations are hot sp for people on the move.

F
tł
dc

Soup Kitchens and Shelters

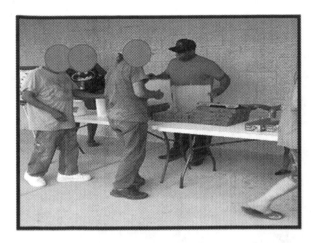

Homeless people are the reason these services are in existence.

Convenience and Grocery Stores

omeless individuals often hang around these establishments due to
·ir high numbers of customers, who more than likely have a few
lars to spare.

Busy Intersections

This is another high-volume traffic area to which some homeless people migrate. Think about the last time you were at a busy intersection; more than likely, there was someone standing outside your vehicle with a sign that said "homeless and hungry." Nine times out of ten, you will not have extra food, but you may have an extra dollar or two. It can really pull on your heart strings to see someone in need right next to you.

A Single Layer of Clothing on a Cold Day

Sometimes one set of clothes is all a person has, and he needs assistance to fight the elements. This person also runs the risk of becoming ill but will not have any money for medicine or the funds to visit a medical facility.

Downtown

Downtown areas have always been a haven for the homeless, which has now become an issue for some city leaders. It does not matter how clean the downtown area is or how many ordinances are passed, it is still an attraction for the homeless. I will discuss city ordinances and the role of government in a later chapter.

Sitting Alone Behind a Restaurant or Store

This is something I have now run across multiple times—on the interstate and when I drive by an establishment. It is hard to describe, because it is so odd. It is like the person is placed in a picture in which he does not belong. He appears in isolation yet his facial expression and body language say "I need help." I discuss one particular situation in the chapter titled "Their Stories."

The Non-Operational Car Wash

This is another sheltered and secluded area where homeless individuals like to hang around.

Railcars and Railroad Areas

I frequently find homeless individuals gathered in these areas. They sometimes use empty boxcars for shelter, especially during winter and on rainy days.

Now my awareness may be different than someone else's, but I can say that I have increased my awareness about the homeless, stranded, and down and out wherever I go, and I am determined to help them. Just as your new car triggered your brain to notice similar vehicles, I hope that my story will now help to stimulate your awareness.

CHAPTER 5
The Good Samaritan

Who is my Neighbor?

The Good Samaritan is a parable told by Jesus and recorded in the Gospel of Luke. Various interpretations of the parable have become part of the mainstream, and today you often hear people say, "I was a good Samaritan today" or "I did my good Samaritan deed."

The parable reads as follows:

> A certain man was going down from Jerusalem to Jericho and he fell among robbers and they stripped him and beat him, went off leaving him half dead. And by chance a certain priest was going down on that road and when he saw him, he passed by on the other side. And likewise a Levite also, when he came to the place and saw him, passed by on the other side. But a certain Samaritan who was on a journey came upon him; and when he saw him,

he felt compassion and came to him, and bandaged up his wounds, pouring oil and wine on them; and he put him on his beast, and brought him to an inn and took care of him. And on the next day he took out two denarii and gave them to the innkeeper and said, "Take care of him and whatever more you spend, when I return, I will pay you." (Luke 10:30–35) (4)

Jesus went on explain who truly had shown mercy toward the man and who was truly his neighbor.

In a later chapter, I will discuss the role of the church and organized religion, but now I want to focus on how the parable relates to the homeless, highlighting a couple of points. Most people would prefer to help those who are in need. As humans, we are equipped with compassion. We may be selective with that compassion, but we all have it in us.

The parable itself does not specifically identify this man who was robbed and left for dead, but based on the people to whom Jesus was speaking; it seems likely that the person resembled his audience. One thing is for sure: the person was in a bad state—physically and probably emotionally. Many who are homeless are broken both physically and emotionally, left on the side of the road of their lives in a half-dead state. This physical and emotional toll may have been inflicted due to one or more of the following reasons, which we discussed earlier:

Economics
- o Rising unemployment
- o Rising health-care costs
- Housing (bad mortgages)

- Natural disasters
- Lack of funding at the local, state, and federal levels
- Domestic violence
- Mental health issues
- Disabilities
- Depression

A homeless person may be on the side of the road of his life, and several things may happen as he interacts with others. Many will pass by with no reaction or emotion toward the individual. Others will have compassion in their hearts and will find a way to help. Some may help by giving some money, buying a meal, or donating to a local charity. A few people may follow-up with the person that they encountered, while others may not (out of sight out of mind). Some may leave the situation feeling good, because they will say they did a good deed. In other words, "I was a Good Samaritan today," or "I did my good Samaritan deed today." Jesus's focus was not just on feeling good about our actions but on understanding the reasons and purpose of why we would help someone.

The question we have to ask is, did we help because the person was a family member or a friend, or for self-gratification? The interesting thing about the parable of the Good Samaritan was that the Samaritan's act was not a singular, feel-good act, but an act of compassion to make sure the person was all right. In all fairness to those who may not make any gesture to help, they may have good reasons—real or perceived. As I mentioned earlier, here are a few reasons some may choose not to interact with someone who is homeless:

- They are criminals.
- They are con artists.
- They are lazy and don't want to work.

- They are drug addicts and winos.
- They are mentally ill.
- They are disabled.

Based on past interactions (as I described earlier), some feel a distrust that makes it not worth the effort to help someone in need. Another interesting thing about this parable is that the parties chose to help or not to help. There was the Levite and the priest who, by the audience's standards, should have had the most compassion and understanding. The Samaritan was considered an outcast and inferior, but he still showed more compassion and understanding than those who were accepted by society. Those who were expected to help left the man on the side of the road and neglected his needs. What Jesus was telling his audience was that a neighbor is more than a family member or someone who is similar to you; it is anyone who shows compassion but expects nothing in return. Among the things that people in the world love about the United States are the words of poet Emma Lazarus written on the Statue of Liberty:

> Give me your tired, your poor, your huddled masses yearning to breathe free, the wretched refuse of your teeming shore. Send these, the homeless, tempest-tost to me; I lift my lamp beside the golden door!

Those words epitomize the parable of the Good Samaritan. However, many things can happen in someone's daily life to make those words tough to believe. As I go around helping the homeless in different states, I sometimes ask myself if I am showing true compassion.

I know I care, and my heart does ache when I see people who are homeless, stranded, or down and out. I do my best to have a conversation with each person as I want to know his story and see if there is anything else that I can do. I am aware that, unlike those who are in close proximity to my residence, there are some people I may never see again in this lifetime and may not know their overall fate. I have to question myself on occasion to make sure my heart is in the right place.

Since I truly believe we should love our neighbors as we love ourselves, I hope that what I do does give meaning to the lives of those I encounter.

CHAPTER 6

The Government's Role in Helping the Homeless

There are a lot of people who regard the role of government and the effectiveness of most government programs with skepticism. A good portion of the country feels that the government has failed in the following key areas: the economy, job creation, protecting the environment, and security. Some say that the government does not do enough, while others believe it does too much. It all depends on what you expect the government to do. The government is for the people and is responsible to the people. When I speak about the government, I am referring to all levels—federal, state and local. Each segment has major budget constraints, political challenges, and an uncertainty about its ability to meet all the needs of society. I would like to briefly explore these three areas of government and see how they are tackling homelessness in this country.

Federal Government

We often hear the phrases "social programs" and "entitlements" when we turn on the television or radio. One group of people claims that spending is out of control, while another group states that not enough is being spent to help the social fabric of the country. Our federal government spent about 59 percent of the federal budget on entitlement programs in 2015.

Below is a breakdown of that spending:

	Welfare programs and other entitlements 10%
Social Security 26%	Medicare, Medicaid and other health-care programs 24%

Source: Office of Management and Budget.

These federal programs, and similar ones at the state and local levels, make up the safety net in our country. Here are a few of the federal government programs designed to help the homeless:

Department of Housing and Urban Development (HUD)

(The Hearth Act)

Continuum of Care (CoC) Program
http://portal.hud.gov/hudportal/HUD?src=/hudprograms/continuumofcare

Emergency Solutions Grant Program
https://www.hudexchange.info/programs/esg/

Rural Housing Stability Assistance Program (RHSP)
http://portal.hud.gov/hudportal/HUD?src=/hudprograms/
rural-housing

Emergency Shelter Grant Program
http://portal.hud.gov/hudportal/HUD?src=/hudprograms/esg

Base Realignment and Closure Program (BRAC)
https://www.hudexchange.info/programs/brac/

HUD Veterans Affairs Supportive Housing Program (HUD-VASH)
http://portal.hud.gov/hudportal/HUD?src=/program_offices/
public_indian_housing/programs/hcv/vash

Department of Health and Human Services (HHS)

Health Care for the Homeless
http://www.bphc.hrsa.gov/

Targeted Homeless Assistance Programs
http://www.hhs.gov/programs/social-services/homelessness/grants/
index.html#targeted

Services in Supportive Housing (SSH)
http://www.samhsa.gov/homelessness-programs-resources/
grant-programs-services/gbhi-program

Basic Center Program
http://www.acf.hhs.gov/fysb/resource/bcp-fact-sheet

Transition Living Program for Older Homeless Youth
http://www.acf.hhs.gov/fysb/programs/runaway-homeless-youth/
programs/transitional-living

Cooperative Agreement to Benefit Homeless Individuals (CABHI)
http://www.samhsa.gov/grants/grant-announcements/sm-16-007

Department of Veteran Affairs (VA)

Veterans Homeless Prevention Demonstration Programs (VHPD)
http://www.va.gov/homeless/nchav/research/program-specific-research/
VHPD-evaluation.asp

VA Compensated Work Therapy (CWT)
http://www.va.gov/health/cwt/

VA's Healthcare for Homeless Veterans Programs (HCHV)
http://www.va.gov/HOMELESS/HCHV.asp

VA's Homeless Patient Aligned Care Teams (HPACTs) Program
http://www.va.gov/homeless/h_pact.asp

VA's Homeless Veteran's Dental Program
http://www.va.gov/HOMELESS/dental.asp

Project Challenge (Community Homeless Assessment Local Education
and Networking Groups)
http://www.va.gov/HOMELESS/chaleng.asp

State and Local Governments

The role played by state and local governments is an interesting one. I
was speaking to a homeless gentleman one Saturday, and he asked me
when the fifteenth day of month was. I told him that it was a week from
Sunday. He had to appear in court on that day. I replied that I didn't
think that it was possible to go to court on a Sunday, and he insisted that
was the date on his citation. He pulled the citation out of his pocket;

the date wasn't the fifteenth but the sixteenth. My shock came when I noticed why he had been cited: "begging." That was the actual word written on the citation. The police had given him the citation, and he was upset.

What this example highlights is the dual role faced by most state and local governments. They want to help the homeless but at the same time are constantly looking for ways to increase their revenue through beautification and revitalization efforts that will attract and retain businesses. Governments need tax revenue to cover their expenses. While the federal and state governments have the ability to generate revenue through payroll taxes and other types of income taxes, local governments typically do not have this luxury.

Local government revenues are driven through tourism, property taxes, occupancy taxes (hotel stays), and sales taxes. Each of these items is what I like to call a choice tax. In other words, if you do not want to pay such taxes, you have the ability to move, not purchase, or not stay where the tax occurs. The same applies to businesses, which have the same rights. Businesses and citizens never want to pay more than their fair share in each of these areas. The hotel cannot pay an occupancy tax if it has no guests. Guests will not stay at a hotel in a high-crime area or where they feel is unsafe. Local government has to make sure that it provides safe, clean areas where businesses can thrive. Without the tax revenue, that can become a difficult task. What are some local governments doing about it? Several cities have passed local ordinances to curb the soliciting of money and goods from strangers without licenses. I do understand the challenges that many cities face.

About ten years ago, the National Law Center on Homelessness & and Poverty and the National Coalition of Homelessness issued a report called "A Dream Denied: The Criminalization of Homelessness in U.S. Cities," which declared these twenty cities as the meanest toward the homeless:

Anchorage, Alaska

Atlanta, Georgia

Austin, Texas

Chicago, Illinois

Dallas, Texas

Flagstaff, Arizona

Houston, Texas

Las Vegas, Nevada

Lawrence, Kansas

Little Rock, Arkansas

Los Angeles, California

New York, New York

Phoenix, Arizona

Pittsburgh, Pennsylvania

San Antonio, Texas

San Francisco, California

San Juan, Puerto Rico

Santa Monica, California

Sarasota, Florida

Saint Louis, Missouri

More than likely, councilmen and councilwomen in these places were looking to strike a balance by producing ordinances to meet the needs of the city for those in need. I have lived in two of these cities (Little Rock and Atlanta) and visited six (San Antonio, Houston, Dallas, Chicago, Saint Louis, and Pittsburg). I have passed out care packages in Little Rock, Atlanta, and Houston.

As with most things, is there really a true balance? The role of government is to look for ways to meet the needs all of citizens in a prudent and equitable manner. It is an extremely tough challenge, and I applaud all the hardworking servants of the people for the outstanding job that they perform. I realize that government alone cannot solve the problem of the homeless, stranded, and down and out. It takes a multitude of people to come up with the best solutions and the resources to ensure those efforts are driven by a common cause.

CHAPTER 7

Religion's Role in Helping the Homeless

A bit of self-disclosure here: I am a follower of Jesus Christ (i.e., a Christian), and therefore I believe the Bible is God's inspired Word and that it is infallible. I am also a human resources professional, and I understand that to be effective in my job, I have to look beyond my own personal beliefs and be consistent and fair as prescribed by the law and the rules that govern my profession. In an earlier chapter I discussed the Good Samaritan parable from the Gospel of Luke. That parable is applicable to all religions and all faiths. Similarly, variations of the Golden Rule—i.e., to treat others the way you want to be treated—can be found in numerous religions. I look at it as the foundation of why we choose to help or not help others.

Here are several interpretations of the Golden Rule from various faiths:

Christianity

"All things whatsoever ye would that man should do to you, do ye so to them; for this is the law and the prophets" (Matthew 7:12).

"Do to others as you would have them do to you" (Luke 6:31).

Confucianism

"Do not do to others what you would not like yourself. Then there will be no resentment against you, either in the family or in the state" (Analect 12:2).

Buddhism

"Hurt not others in ways that you yourself would find hurtful" (Udana-Varga 5,1).

Hinduism

"This is the sum of duty; do naught onto others what you not have them do unto you" (Mahabharata 5,1517).

Islam

"No one of you is a believer until he desires for his brother that which he desires for himself" (Sunnah).

Judaism

"What is hateful to you, do not do to your fellowman. This is the entire Law, all the rest is commentary" (Talmud, Shabbat 3id)

Taoism

"Regard your neighbors gain as your gain, and your neighbor's loss as your own loss" (Tai Shang Kan Yin P'ien).

Zoroastrianism

"That nature alone is good which refrains from another whatsoever is not good for itself" (Dadisten-Idiik, 94,5).

Jesus was asked this question by one of the religious leaders of the day: "Teacher, which commandment in the law is the greatest?"

> Jesus said to him, "Love the Lord your God with all your heart, with all your soul, and with all your mind. This is the first and the greatest commandment. The second is like it, Thou shall love thy neighbor as thyself, on these two commandments hang all the laws and the prophets on them." (Matthew 22:36–40)

Based upon this snapshot of several different religions and using the Golden Rule as a foundation, it is very apparent that most religious people want to help those in need and that they have compassion for those individuals. What does each religion say about the homeless, stranded, and down and out?

Christianity

The Bible lists several verses that instruct believers on their responsibility to the homeless, stranded, and down and out.

> And if thy brother be waxen poor, and fallen in decay with thee, then shalt relieve him: yea, though he be a stranger or a sojourner that he may live with the. Take thou no usury of him, or increase, but fear thy God; that they brother may live with thee. (Leviticus 25:35–36)

> "Is it not to deal thy bread to the hungry, and that thou bring the poor that are cast out to thy house? When thou seest the naked, that thou cover him, and that thou hide not thyself from thine own flesh? (Isaiah 58:7)

Then shall the King say unto them on his right hand, Come ye blessed of my Father, inherit the kingdom prepared for you from the foundation of the world. For I was hungered, and ye gave me meat. I was thirsty, and ye gave me drink. I was a stranger, and ye took me in; naked, and ye clothed me. I was sick, and ye visited me. I was in prison and ye come unto me.

Then shall the righteous answer him, saying, Lord, when saw we thee hungered and fed thee? Or thirst, and gave thee drink? When saw we thee a stranger, and took thee in? Or naked and clothed thee? Or when saw we thee sick, or in prison and came unto thee? And the King shall answer and say unto them, Verily I say unto you, inasmuch as ye have done it unto one of the least of them my brethren, ye have done it unto me. (Matthew 25:34–40)

Jesus replied and said, "A certain man was going down from Jerusalem to Jericho, and he fell among robbers, and they stripped him and beat him, went off leaving him half dead. And by chance a certain priest was going down on that road and when he saw him, he passed by on the other side. And likewise a Levite also, when he came to the place and saw him, passed by on the other side. But a certain Samaritan, who was on a journey came upon him; and when he saw him, he felt compassion and came to him, and bandaged up his wounds, pouring oil and wine on them; and he put him on his beast, and brought him to an inn and took care of him. And on the next day he took out two denarii and gave them to the innkeeper and said, 'Take care of him and whatever more you spend, when I come again, I will repay thee.' Which now of these three, thinkest thou, was neighbor unto him that fell among the thieves? "And he said, "He that showed mercy on him." Then said Jesus unto him, "Go and thou likewise." (Luke 10:30–37)

For whosoever exalteth himself shall be abased; and he that humbleth himself shall be exalted. Then said he also to him that abased him, when thou makest a dinner or a supper, call not thy friend, nor thy brethren, neither they kinsmen, nor they rich neighbors, lest they also bid thee again, and recompense be made thee. But when thou makest a feast call the poor, the maimed, the lame, the blind; and thou shalt be blessed; for they cannot recompense thee: for thou shalt be recompensed at the resurrection of the just. (Luke 14:11–14)

Defend the poor and fatherless; do justice to the afflicted and needy. (Psalm 82:3

He that hath pity upon the poor lendeth unto the Lord; and that which he hath given will he pay him again. (Proverbs 19:17)

Islam

They (are those who) fulfill (their) vows and fear a day whose evil will be widespread. And they give food in spite of love for it to the needy, orphan and the captive. (Saying) We feed you for the countenance of Allah.

We wish not from your reward or gratitude. (Qur'an 76:7–9)

And your Lord is going to give to you and you will be satisfied. Did he not find you as an orphan and gave (you) refuge? He found you lost and guided (you), He found you poor and made (you) self-sufficient. So as for the orphans do not oppress (him). And for the petitioner do not repel (him). (Surat-Ad-Dhuha 93:5–10)

Confucianism

In a country well governed, poverty is something to be ashamed of, in a country that is badly governed; wealth is something to be ashamed of." (Confucius)

Buddhism

Have compassion for all beings, rich and poor alike, each have their suffering, some too much, others too little. (Buddha)

Judaism

And when you reap the harvest of your land, thou shalt not wholly reap the corners of thy field, neither shalt thou gather the gleaning of thy harvest. And thou shalt not glean thy vineyard, neither shalt thou gather every grape of the vineyard, thou shalt leave them for the poor and strangers; I am the Lord your God. (Leviticus 19:9–10)

Hinduism

> He who feeds a stranger and a tired traveler with joy attain infinite religious merit. (Mahabharata XIII 7.7)

Zoroastrianism

> The power and glory of God is given to those who give protection to those in need. (YAN 27.13, Avesta)

As you can see, all the religions that I have listed have some foundational spiritual truth focused on helping those in need. With everything from soup kitchens to clothing outlets, people of various faiths have been helping the needy for centuries. Sometimes the assistance starts in local communities and then expands to national and international missionary work. People of faith, and especially in the Christian church, have worked with federal, state, and local authorities to make up some of the shortfalls that governments have encountered in their quest to help the homeless, stranded, and down and out.

The church has played a major role in providing disaster relief and in mobilizing resources to help those in need. For example, on August 23, 2005, in the midst of Hurricane Katrina, churches throughout the South set up command centers. They worked with state and local governments as well as utilities, hospitals, and civic organizations to provide relief to the citizens of their communities. Local churches provided food, shelter, and clothing to those who were in need.

One challenge some churches face is having enough cash. Most churches are dependent upon their congregations, relying on them to give enough in tithes and offerings to fund internal and external activities. If the needs inside the church are so great that the funding can sustain only internal programs, then outside activities, such as helping the homeless, cannot be funded or implemented.

Speaking as a church deacon and trustee, I can tell you that it is a challenge to make sure you help your congregation first, which we call our local benevolence, and then move outward with a large benevolence ministry. Some larger churches or those with greater resources do have the ability to have specific ministries, such as a food ministry, shelter ministry, or a vehicle ministry that can support the homeless.

One difference between the government and the church is that the church was built on the principle of a divine being with compassion on the less fortunate. Ultimately, the political will of the people determines what the government will do.

I definitely believe that organized religion should be the leader and driver in making sure that those who are less fortunate are not forgotten and that this is one of the main tenets of its mission.

CHAPTER 8

The Role of Charitable Organizations in Helping the Homeless

I wish I could name every international, national, and local organization whose sole purpose is to help those who are homeless. I have seen a lot of things in my life but nothing as amazing as the various groups and the individuals who work and volunteer to help. Their purpose is pretty straightforward: they want to help those who are in need.

Interestingly enough, each organization has a different mission. One agency may be centered on providing food, another agency may provide shelter, yet another may help people find suitable work, while a different organization may provide health-care services. Some of these organizations mirror certain government agencies in their work, as they may deal with only veterans or substance abusers or victims of domestic violence. As I have researched and gotten a chance to see some of these great organizations at work, it is apparent that they face a common challenge: funding.

Funding is extremely important for these organizations and unfortunately they are in a battle to get it. Although we may scrutinize how our tax dollars are spent, we are still obligated to pay taxes. Encouraged by a higher spiritual calling, people of faith give offerings or pay some type of tithe. Most have varying views when it comes to donating to social and civic organizations. Some want to see what was done with previous funding while others want certainty that the funds will be utilized for their stated purpose. All of these are legitimate inquiries. The scrutiny for most charitable organizations happens before funding is allocated.

Sources of Funding

Charitable organizations have three main sources of funding: 1) grants, 2) direct donations and services, and 3) corporate donations.

Grants

These funds come from traditional foundations, family foundations, and businesses foundations.

1) Traditional foundation grants are funding sources that are tied to specific criteria that must be met, such as providing services in a certain area or helping a designated group. There is usually a standard application and sometimes an interview. Although the process can be very tedious, the thoroughness and consistency allows for transparency. Government grants can be done at the federal, state, or local level of government and are usually more accessible than grants from family or business foundations.

2) Family foundation grants are usually driven by the wishes of the person who established the foundation. Below is a list of some of the largest foundations in the United States:
   - Bill & Melinda Gates Foundation
   - The Ford Foundation
   - The Robert Wood Johnson Foundation

- The William and Flora Hewlett Foundation
- W. K. Kellogg Foundation
- The David and Lucile Packard Foundation
- The Andrew W. Mellon Foundation

3) Business foundation grants are usually tied to the interests of the corporation. Several major Fortune 100 and 500 organizations for which I've worked donated funds to aid the communities they served or to highlight a specific issue that had a direct (or sometimes indirect) effect on the business.

Direct Donations and Services

From the Red Kettle Program to United Way Campaigns, social and civic organizations have the ability to initiate funding drives for special causes or for day-to-day operations. Some of the largest direct donations come from businesses in the form of individual payroll deductions. These donations can be tax deductible for the individual. Major groups like the United Way represent several other charitable organizations. The contributor can determine how much or what percent of their contribution they would like to go to a specific charity or let the United Way choose how to disburse the funds.

Many of the agencies represented by the United Way make presentations to organizations or businesses in their communities. In the 1990s, while I was living in the Atlanta area, I began training to be in the United Way board of director's pool, handling nonprofit disbursements of funds to the greater Atlanta area. Unfortunately, due to time constraints, I was unable to finish the program. But I gained an understanding of the legal and fiduciary responsibilities through the training that board of directors and the individual agencies within United Way has toward the donors and the organizations. Transparency is important in these organizations and they strive to ensure that the activities are clear to all.

Some social and civic organizations have the ability to sell certain services to earn revenue, but this is usually at a minor level.

Corporate Donations

Donations from businesses are separate from grants and can be either financial or services of value. Financially, the funds can match what employees donate to a certain organization or a separate payment entirely. Similar to business grants, most businesses try to contribute to those organizations that may have a direct or indirect impact on their interests.

Challenges in Funding

As it is for the government and religious organizations, funding for civic and social organizations is a huge concern. While the government and religious organizations may have to cut back on or stop donating to certain programs, social and civic organizations are more tied to the end users of their services. Shortfalls in funding have a direct impact. Given the limited number of funding dollars, all organizations have to show the true value of the services they provide. People want to see if they are good and true stewards of the funds they receive. Each organization must constantly make the case that it has integrity and is worthy of support.

When the United Way of America was rocked by scandal in the early 1990s, it had a rippling effect—not only for those under the United Way banner but for all nonprofits around the country. Skepticism slipped in, and the integrity of anyone looking for funding for a good cause was challenged. The issue was not whether the purpose was sound but if the organizations had hired people who were of good judgment and character. Who within an organization had true business acumen? Were those in charge going do the right thing? People wanted to know if the funds would be used to support someone's lifestyle. Unfortunately, those questions will continue to linger, especially during a time when the economy has slowed down, and funds are limited.

Smaller organizations that may not have big name appeal sometimes can be the ones left out of funding disbursements. Lack of understanding about how to write a grant proposal, where to seek funds, and how to develop financial strategies are a huge factor and challenge for those securing funds, and this has a direct impact on the end user. As I stated earlier in this chapter, there are many wonderful people and organizations doing tremendous work, especially in the area of taking care of the homeless. If someone does not believe the leader of an organization has the integrity to do what is right, then the funding may not go to the organization. It does not matter if it is the Atlanta Symphony Orchestra or L.OV.E.'s (Lauderdale Outreach and Voluntary Effort, Inc.) Kitchen in Meridian, people want to make sure that there is good stewardship in place.

What does this mean for the homeless, stranded, and down and out? The funding to help those who are less fortunate definitely competes with other worthy causes. At a time when much is dependent upon the hearts and minds of those who are willing to make the donations, so much uncertainty can limit the impact of giving. Social and civic organizations alike are judged when it comes to helping the homeless, stranded, and down and out.

If you have the perception that homeless individuals fit into one or more of the categories listed below, then you probably will not want to donate to an organization that supports them:

- They are criminals.
- They are con artists.
- They are lazy and don't want to work.
- They are drug addicts and alcoholics.
- They are mentally ill.
- They are physically disabled.

It is a personal choice. However, I know that the wonderful individuals I have come across—and the many hundreds I have read about and researched—are doing a wonderful job, and they need all of the support (financially and morally) that they can get. The end user (the homeless, stranded, and down and out) definitely can use the assistance.

CHAPTER 9

Teaching a Man to Fish

Give a man a fish, and you feed him for the day. Teach a man to fish, and you feed him for a lifetime. (Chinese proverb)

Many of us have heard these words dozens of times; we may have said them ourselves. There have been many different explanations of the statement. It has been quoted and misquoted, and its origin has been misidentified as well. I myself have interpreted this saying in a few ways:

- Provide for a man, and he will look for you to continue to provide for him, but teach a man how to provide for himself and he will become self-sufficient.
- Feed a man and he will only be fed for a short period of time, but teach a man how to feed himself, and it will have a longer impact.
- If you feed a man, it will have a long-lasting, negative impact on him. However, if you teach him how to feed himself, that will lead to a more positive long-term outcome for him.

As I work with the homeless, stranded, and down and out, this old proverb has given me mixed emotions (anger and empathy) and left me with two questions: (1) if I help you, will you help yourself? (2) if I help you, can you help yourself?

If I Help You, Will You Help Yourself?

Let's examine the first question. If you work at a place or provide a service that helps those in need, then you may ask yourself the following question: does the person want to help himself? How often have you seen individuals holding signs similar to these:

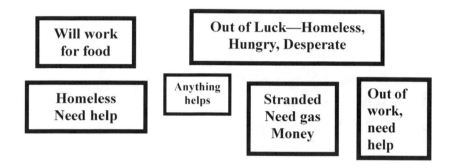

After seeing such signs, most people's compassion will kick in, and they will give whatever they can to help that individual's situation. More likely than not, people do not ask how this will help the situation or wonder what the individual will do after he receives their assistance. So it often appears that there are more of us feeding than teaching to fish.

Most of the people I have helped are in Mississippi, where I live. I have had the opportunity to observe some individuals for months. I've not only observed them, I've also sat down and talked with them. There are individuals who have been soliciting handouts for more than a year. Each day that they are fed means one more day when no one is steering them in the direction of self-sufficiency. As one person told me, "You can make between $25 and $50 a day and then go eat at L.O.V.E.'s Kitchen for free and stay at that Salvation Army or under the bridge.

Why is there a need to work?" That was pretty astonishing, but he was being truthful.

Now everyone cannot stop what he is doing in his own personal life and teach. Some individuals will tell you that they never give money to a person who says they are hungry, but they will buy them a meal if they are really hungry. I have heard the same thing said regarding individuals who are stranded and need gas to get to their destination; they will not give money but will purchase the gas.

In all honesty, most of us would accept something of value for free with no strings attached or if no effort were needed. If you saw a fairly healthy-looking individual week after week or month after month on the street corner asking for money, at some point you might say to yourself, *Enough is enough.* Now if you had been giving him money then you may want to get on a loud speaker and tell others, "Please do not give that individual any money." You wonder if the individual wants to help himself.

Now in all fairness, unemployment benefits can last up to twenty-six weeks, so it is plausible for someone in a tough economy to be in a bind for a number of months. I am not suggesting that all individuals out on the street are not seeking some type of employment. I understand that the funds from unemployment may not be adequate enough to keep someone from becoming homeless in some instances. I do believe people are willing to help someone who is truly making an effort to remove himself from his current situation. Most homeless people I have encountered truly want to do so.

If I Help You, Can You Help Yourself?

For me, the interesting thing about this question was that I had to take my emotions out in order to answer it. Once I was able to do that, I had a different response. I went back to the Chinese proverb: "Give a man a fish and you feed him for the day, teach a man to fish and you feed him for a life time."

I have been a human resources professional for twenty-seven years, certified in the field for twenty-one years through the Society of Human Resources Management. I have worked in several Fortune 100 and 500 companies and have a very good understanding of people's talents, motivations, and behaviors. I have been an ordained deacon in the Baptist church for the last eleven years and a Sunday school teacher for more than twenty-five years. I have had more training regarding people, people practices, and business than I care to mention. The one thing that all of this experience has taught me is that everyone does not learn in the same manner, have the same motivation, or play on a level field.

When I began this journey of helping others, my goal was to be a bridge between those in need and the agencies that provide the help. I will discuss my purpose in a later chapter of the book. But the question, "if I help you, can you help yourself" has become a lot clearer for me as it relates to some of the homeless individuals that I have met. The answer to the question is yes and no.

I believe that most homeless individuals can help themselves. They have the competency and capability to do so. (This excludes individuals who are genuinely physically or mentally unable.) However, my profession has taught me a lot about how individuals are able to help themselves.

Most people wonder why homeless individuals do not seek employment. Here are a few challenges in this area:

1. They may not have a valid driver's license or a photo ID. If you are seeking employment, this is needed for the Immigration and Naturalization (I-9) Process.
2. They may not have a birth certificate or Social Security card (the most popular documents). This too is needed for the I-9 Process and also to get a driver's license or a photo ID.
3. A criminal record could affect their ability to find employment.
4. The lack of a stable work history could eliminate them from consideration.
5. They have do not have any suitable clothes for an interview.
6. They do not have a telephone number to list under contact information.
7. They may not be able to pass a pre-hire drug screen.
8. They may not have transportation to get to an interview or work.
9. Hygiene could be an issue (because they are not able to bathe, brush teeth, comb hair, etc.).
10. They have no suitable references.

These are just some factors that could affect a person's ability to fish (feed himself). Usually, when we think about this proverb, particularly the second portion—"teach a man to fish, and you feed him for a lifetime"—we often think about teaching someone a trade. Most people do have some skills or capabilities that they have used inside and outside the work environment. Unfortunately, if they can't get past the preliminary phase, then they will never have a chance to present those skills or capabilities. Although agencies and institutions try to help individuals seeking employment opportunities, they may be located far away. In addition, many homeless have given up on the possibility of working and seek the satisfaction of being fed at that moment.

On an unlevel playing field, where all things and people are not equal, the best man or woman gets the opportunity regardless of race, sex, color, national origin, age, or social status. Now before someone calls me delusional, the aspect that makes the field unlevel is that everyone may not have the skills and abilities needed to create value or may not have been in an environment that best develops the values and behaviors needed. This is the situation for most people who are homeless.

All homeless stories are not the same as Chris Gardner's as documented in *The Pursuit of Happyness*. I think if you were to ask Gardner "if I help you, will you help yourself?" and "if I help you, can you help yourself?" the answer to both questions would be yes. The many that are helping the homeless need a paradigm shift to find ways to teach people to fish, which is the long-term goal. But at the same time, we cannot forget to feed them, which is the immediate need. That is my quest and my mission. The next time you see some of these signs, how will you react?

Homeless
Need
help

Homeless
Will work
for food

I am out
of work,
need help

CHAPTER 10

Their Stories

I have run across some interesting stories in my travels assisting and learning about the homeless, stranded, and down and out. My goal always is to talk with every individual I come across as I offer a care package and explain who I am and describe my purpose. In this chapter, I will share a few of the more interesting stories, using only initials or nicknames.

Quite a few individuals who were homeless have prayed for me and some have asked me to pray for them. More people have prayed for me than I have prayed for in the public square. Several have cried, and overwhelming number have hugged me as if I were a long lost brother. The individuals I have come across are of different races, genders and ages—single, married, and family groups. Some spoke very eloquently; others may have had limited education. Some were disabled; others seemed to be in excellent physical shape.

Pride is one of the key character traits that can be affected when you are homeless. I have come across some people who refused any assistance and also those who show extreme humility. Here are a few of their stories.

Popeye

White male, 67

Driving through Gulfport, Mississippi, I saw a gentleman pushing a wheelchair across busy Highway 49. He called himself Popeye, and he was an elderly gentleman who was hurt on an offshore rig twenty-plus years ago. He'd had open heart surgery and had been to prison on numerous occasions. He said with a proud look that his focus was now on God's will for his life.

Popeye told me that he was not well educated, and he knew few words with more than four letters. He had a car but it was not running, and if he could get enough money to put a motor in it, it would be a good car. He pointed to a vacant lot off of Highway 49 and told me that he wanted to find the owner so he could set up a tent and have church services there. He used to work on the oil rigs in the Gulf of Mexico and one day he was injured on the job. Popeye was not able to draw workers' compensation at the time, because the company said he was negligent, but his body had not been right since. The scars on both of his knees looked like something you would see on a former athlete. He said that on some days he could barely walk.

I asked him if the wheelchair he was pushing around was so he could rest his knees. He gave me an emphatic "Hell naw!" and added "I don't need no damn wheelchair to get around; I may sit in it time to time and carry my stuff in it, but I am Popeye and I am strong." He told me that he'd lived a hard life, and some of it was his own doing. He'd fought with family members. He opened his shirt and showed me a scar from a previous heart surgery. Then he said, "But old Popeye is tough;

ask anybody around here about Popeye." He said he hadn't always lived right but God had a plan for him.

He tried his best not to use much profanity, but every now and then a word or two would slip out, and he would apologize. He lived on the streets and in shelters, but he said that God had provided for him and wanted him to go out and spread the good news. In a somber tone, he said, "It is rough out here on these streets but I am going to make it because God has a plan for me."

He was not looking to leave the area and after our forty-five-minute conversation, on the side of Highway 49 as the sun was going down, he asked if I would pray for him. I told him yes. I prayed for him, and he took my care package and told me he was greatly appreciative and asked me to look him up the next time I was in town. I watched as Popeye moved on down the highway with a sense of confidence and pride. His weary body and cracked face told a whole different story.

M

White female, mid-30s

Driving around Meridian, Mississippi, one Saturday morning in late December, I pulled off of the Philadelphia/Airport exit looking for anyone who was in need of help. It was an overcast day and, in all honesty, I was kind of tired. I noticed a woman sitting by herself behind a convenience store. As I turned the car around, she got off the stoop and walked down the street. I pulled my car up to her and told her who I was and what I was doing. She said that she was homeless, and I asked her how she ended up that way.

She said, "I have done some stupid things, just some very stupid things. I have been in Meridian for about 10 years; I use to live in Florida. I was here with my boyfriend and all he did was beat on me and abuse me. He didn't give a damn about me and I shouldn't have followed him around. I thought I was in love, but look at me: I am on the streets. I have just done some stupid things. There are times when I just don't know what I am going to do each day. I am just trying to survive."

She had an extremely embarrassed look on her face as she told me her story. I told her there was nothing to be embarrassed about, that we have all fallen at some point in our lives.

She added, "I have been on drugs, which was stupid, and I'm just a very ugly person now." I told her not to call herself ugly and that she was a beautiful person.

She thanked me and continued, "You can't tell that I use drugs; I am so embarrassed right now sir. It is just very tough out here."

I asked where was she staying, and she pointed back toward the interstate and said she sleeps under the bridges sometimes. I told her about the Salvation Army, and she said, "There is really no place for women to stay. I've been to the Salvation Army, and they gave me money for one night to stay at a hotel, but they only have rooms for the men who are there who work for them, and then they give rooms to women who have children. There is really no place for single women to stay. I have just been so stupid. Did you say that there were some snacks and information about places to stay in the box?"

I said yes, and she thanked me and I watched her depart from my rearview mirror as she headed back to the stoop where she'd been sitting.

It was one of those occasions where I felt my help was inadequate, even though the information in the care package did list various groups that could assist her. I put my car in drive, drove a few yards to turn around, and stopped the car. I began to feel really down about her. I reached in my pocket to see how much extra money I had, as I'd decided to give her some cash beyond what was in the care package. This is something that I usually try not to do since I want individuals to be able to fully utilize all the contents of the package. However, my guilt was so strong—guilt for wishing that I could do more.

I pulled up to the stoop where she was sitting and noticed that she had opened up the care package. I called her over to the car and gave her the extra money. She had opened the can of Vienna sausages and was eating them. She said, "I am so sorry. You just don't know how hungry I am. I really appreciate you helping me today, sir, I am just so hungry."

She looked as if it was her first taste of food in days. I asked if she had been to L.O.V.E.'s Kitchen and she said that she had, during Thanksgiving. I told her they serve breakfast and lunch every day of the week. The impression she left on me that Saturday afternoon still troubles me, and I remember going home and weeping about her situation. Domestic violence, a drug problem, and homelessness had her feeling helpless and had given her very low self-esteem.

I had been looking for her since we met that Saturday, but quite a bit of time had passed before I saw her again. Then one Sunday afternoon, after church, I drove back into the area where I seen her several months earlier, and there she was, behind the store again. I stopped and spoke with her for about a half an hour. She said that she was still homeless but she was able to stay with a couple of friends every now and then, and her goal was to leave the state. She had been to L.OV.E.'s Kitchen on a couple of occasion for meals. I recommended that she reach out to the local shelter for women who have been abused. She assured me that she would. I gave her my card and told her to call me if things seemed too tough to handle.

KT

White male, mid-50s

I met KT off I-20 South, exit 49. KT is what I would describe as stranded which is not uncommon in Meridian. I-20 is a high-volume trucking route that comes through the city, where a number of individuals are dropped off and look to hitchhike to their next destination. KT was one such individual. I pulled off to the side of the overpass, told him who I was and what I was doing, and gave him a care package. His sign read "Stranded and Homeless—want to get to Texas." I asked him where he came from, and he told me his story.

"I have been here about two weeks." KT said. "I caught a ride this far cause I'm trying to get Texas to find work. I worked for a trucking company in Georgia, but the work stopped. I was told there are some companies hiring in Texas, and I am trying to get a ride there. I didn't think I would be here this long but I can't find anybody to give me a ride to Texas. My money has run out, so I've been sleeping under the bridge here, trying to get some money to eat and catch a ride to Texas."

He stood up to talk to me and winced in pain. I asked him what was wrong and if he'd been sitting too long? KT said, "No, my back is really hurting bad and it has been like that for a while. I am thirsty." I told him that there was a bottle of water in the care package, and he opened the box and took the bottle of water out and began to drink it. I asked if he had family in Texas, and he said no. I showed him the information regarding the shelters, food pantries, and clinics in Meridian, and he said thank you, and I departed. Several weeks later, he was back at the exit. Again, he said that no one would give him a ride to Texas. KT had not yet become officially homeless; he was still stranded. Unfortunately as time progresses he will become truly homeless in Meridian, Mississippi.

D

Black female, 58

One Saturday afternoon in February 2016, I crossed paths with a very interesting person. She was wandering up and down the street and I watched her for about twenty minutes before I approached her. It was one of the most interesting and fulfilling encounters I have had. The encounter turned into an emotional mutual prayer session. D is from Greenville, Mississippi, and you can tell the streets have not been kind to her. She is missing several teeth and has patches of her hair missing; she walks with a fast-paced limp and probably could outrun me and some younger folks. She approached my car cautiously, with a wild-eyed look on her face. I introduced myself and asked if she could use some assistance. By the looks people gave us as they drove or walked by, it was apparent that most in the area had seen her around. They seemed to say either what is she doing bothering that man, or what is he doing bothering that woman? It was kind of amusing.

The next twenty minutes were very interesting. She introduced herself, and I told her what was in the care package and about my purpose. She said she needed just a couple of dollars for a ninety-nine-cent cheeseburger from Wendy's. I told her there were a couple of dollars as well as some snacks in the box. She asked me what church I was with, and I told her, and explained that I was not out there on behalf of any church but to follow the purpose given to me by the Lord. She started to cry and told me her story in a high-pitched, rapid tone.

"Lord knows I don't mean no one no harm," she said. "People be jumping on me for no reason. My father use to be a sheriff when I was growing up. This man I use to be with was so mean to me, and he used to just beat on me for no reason, and he gave me the HIV. So now I can't get no man cause he has messed me up. I have been shot before. Can you see that right there?"

She lifted the partial stocking cap that covered only a portion of her hair. She repeated, "People be jumping on me for no reason out here and it is crazy." She began to cry and said that she tried her best to do right by God, but she kept doing the wrong thing. I tried to assure her that we all fall short and that God is a loving God who loves us all. She asked if I would pray for her. I grabbed both of her hands and I began to pray. I grabbed her hand and noticed that she could not fully open her right hand. After I finished praying, I offered her some socks and a ski hat, which I hand out as part of another program, called B&S for Blankets and Socks, that I instituted for the homeless, stranded, and down and out. She started to cry again and said, "You are a good man. No one has ever been this nice to me."

She asked if I was married, and I told her yes. Once again she showed me the physical challenges she faced. She said, "Look at my eye" and raised her eyelid to show me the broken and swollen blood vessels. "I barely can see, and it is hard out here for me. The place I am trying to stay won't be there for long, because the termites are eating it up." With tears rolling out of her eyes, she said, "I am a sinner, but the Lord knows I'm trying to do better." She quoted several scriptures. "I know the Lord can take care of me because he was able to change Paul, and he was able to forgive David after he sinned with Bathsheba, and God called him a man after his own heart."

She said, "I need to pray for you because you are doing God's will, and I need him to protect you, because it is dangerous out here and I don't want anybody to jump you like they have been jumping me." She prayed for me and cried a little bit more and asked if I would come around again. I told her she would see my white truck driving around and that was a promise. I put her care package, hat, and socks in a Wal-Mart bag so she could carry them easily. I watched her walk away, hoping that she felt some normalcy after our conversation and mutual prayer session.

R.A. and J.A.

White male, mid-50s; white female, mid-50s

One Sunday night in March, I was leaving the Wal-Mart store in the Bonita Lake area in Meridian. I noticed three individuals on the corner. One was sitting on the bench and the other two were standing nearby. I thought I knew all three of them, so I decided to pass them by since I had figured that I had previously given them care packages. As I drew closer, I realized that I had helped the gentleman sitting on the bench, but I had not seen the other individuals (a man and a woman) before. I wanted to stop and speak with them, but unfortunately a policeman was right behind me, and an awkward turn probably would have meant a ticket. I continued to drive for about a mile and then turned around. When I arrived back at the location, the gentleman I'd helped before was still sitting on the bench, but the man and woman had walked several hundred feet away. They were sitting in front of a closed restaurant. I drove up to them and asked if they needed assistance.

The man was R.A., and his wife was J.A. He said, "Yes but I need to tell you why my wife and I are out here." Three weeks earlier they had been passing through Meridian, when they decided to pull off of I-20/59 to do some shopping at Wal-Mart. His wife walked out of the store first and was approached by a man (whom they later identified as Archie, a homeless man in the area). J.A. said that the man came to their car and asked for a ride. She told him "My husband will be out of the store shortly, and he can help you." The man forced her into the car and made her drive around the corner, where he threatened to kill her and then took her in the woods. J.A. said that the man was going to rape her, but some other people happened to be walking through the woods. He let her go but took her car and told her he would kill her if she said anything.

R.A. went to the police and reported the crime. Without their vehicle, they were stranded in Meridian, and they had been trying to get to Pensacola, Florida. He and his wife had depleted their funds and had been asking for handouts for three weeks. About a week after the incident, another homeless person told him where he could find his vehicle. It was non-operational, and he had it towed to the shop, but it would cost $600 to repair.

"It makes no sense for them to damage my vehicle," he said. "My wife has kidney problems, and she is still afraid for me to leave her sight. God will deal with the evil man, and he will eventually be punished."

"I don't know why this man wanted to harm me," J.A. said, as tears rolled down from her eyes. "I never did anything to him. I don't even know him."

The police told R.A. that since his wife let the man into the car it was not considered a carjacking, and since he did not physically harm her, it was not an assault.

"We have now had on the same clothes for three weeks and have been out here seeking help. I never dreamed of something like this happening. Both of us have doctor's appointments coming up, and my wife has bad kidney problems as she has peed on herself three times." R.A.'s voice grew angrier. "God is going to punish that man for what he did to my wife. And this man …" R.A. pointed to the gentleman who was sitting on the bench. "He has caught me on the wrong day. I will hurt him if he disrespects my wife again!"

I asked him what had happened. "My wife needed to rest her legs due to her kidney problem," R.A. said, "and this man tells her that she cannot sit there, because he had the bench for another thirty minutes, and he begins to yell at her to get off of the bench. I am the wrong one for him to do this to. You don't insult my wife. He does not own that damn bench."

I told R.A. to calm down and asked if he wanted me to pray for him and his wife. He said that would be fine. I grabbed R.A.'s right hand with my left hand and J.A.'s left hand with my right hand through my passenger window, as they held each other's hands, and I prayed for them. I saw the two of them around for another couple of weeks. R.A. said his family was going to wire him some money. I asked J.A. how she was holding up; she said she had been sick the last couple of days. They had been to L.O.V.E.'s Kitchen to eat and had visited a walk in clinic. I have not seen them since, so I assume they eventually fixed their car and headed to Florida.

These are just a few of the hundreds of stories that I have heard.

CHAPTER 11
My Purpose

What is my purpose? Why am I writing this book? My purpose was born out of my faith and my belief that God's purpose for me is to find ways to utilize my talents and knowledge to help others. This is not some new revelation designed only for me; nor does it mean that others have not been given a similar purpose in life. Determining a purpose beyond ourselves is a great challenge. We all seek to maximize our talents in ways that are fulfilling and rewarding and hopefully in ways from which others can benefit. However, our immediate purpose still starts with us.

I once worked for a Fortune 100 Company that taught us the following economic lesson: the butcher, the baker, and the candlestick maker had a purpose, and that purpose started with how they could maximize their talents and goods—first for themselves and then in a way that profited others. That is the nature of entrepreneurship and, unfortunately, how most people view their giving, i.e., what's in it for me? The opposite viewpoint of this is true servitude. How can I help others unconditionally? The Salvation Army represents the opposite viewpoint. This movement, started by William Booth in the 1800s, was built upon Booth's faith in the church and his belief in the teachings and directions of Jesus Christ. That became his purpose. There are several key factors that have driven me to do what I am currently doing. They are 1) scripture, 2) asking what I've done to have an impact on other people's lives and 3) how I want to be remembered.

Scripture

The Bible has guided me in my quest to help and understand the homeless. I think about all the good and the bad that is going on and I ask myself if I am contributing to the "good" in a positive way and finding ways to eliminate the "bad." Several key scriptures have led me in my purpose to help the homeless, stranded, and down and out:

- The Parable of the Good Samaritan (Luke: 10:30–37)
- The Golden Rule (Matthew 7:12)
- Faith and Works Together (James 2:14–18)

My Purpose as Outlined in the Parable of the Good Samaritan

As I discussed in a previous chapter, the parable of the Good Samaritan describes a man who had been beaten and left for dead on the side of the road. Several individuals saw the man lying on the side of the road but only one person stopped to help—the most unlikely individual to help a stranger according to the standards of society at that time. The individuals who should have helped passed him by. I asked myself if am I so religious that I show favoritism toward some and do not help everyone. This is a sin as outlined in James 2:1–9.

Jesus spoke about the Good Samaritan after he was asked what is required to inherit eternal life. Jesus asked what is written in the law. The person responded, "Love the Lord your God with all your heart, with all your soul, and with all your strength, and with your entire mind, and love your neighbor as yourself." Jesus said he had answered correctly, but the gentlemen wanted a more complete explanation; he asked, "Who is my neighbor?"

The parable taught me that everyone is my neighbor regardless of race, sex, religion, national origin, age, disability, or sexual orientation, or whether the person is a saint, sinner, Jew, Gentile, or has any other real or perceived differences that separate individuals in a negative way. An individual once asked me if I ever get scared or nervous about going up to certain people to offer help. I told him yes, on occasion, and that it was human nature to have reservations when approaching strangers in certain areas or at certain times of the day. I explained that it would be a lie to say that I don't survey a situation before I approach anyone. I may sit and watch someone for thirty to forty-five minutes before I approach.

As I told him, I am definitely not a holier than thou person, but I do pray for guidance in most situations. Every individual is not guided to do things the same way, and I definitely could view the Good Samaritan parable in a different light if it had been introduced to me in a non-scriptural way. I recognize the fear of physical harm that many may feel. As I stated previously, such perceptions (see below) of the homeless are understandable.

Perceptions of the Homeless

They are criminals.

They are con artists.

They are lazy and don't want to work.

They are drug addicts and winos.

They are mentally ill.

They are disabled.

But scripture has been my guidance, including this verse that supports my understanding of helping a neighbor or a stranger: "Be not forgetful to entertain strangers; for thereby some have entertained angels without knowing it." (Hebrews 13:2).

My Purpose as Outlined in the Golden Rule

The chapter on the role of religious organizations described how the Golden Rule—"Do unto others as you would have them do unto you" (Luke 6:31)—has universal meaning and is found in several religions.

I did not have a Chris Gardener moment, but I, like so many others, have been without a job before (purely my fault). My situation was pretty tough. My oldest daughter was about to begin college, and all of my family's health-care coverage was through my employer. I could not pay my mortgage; eventually my severance, which was my lifeline, was depleted. I was not able to draw unemployment due to the severance, so things got ugly during the next six months. I often ask myself what if I had been in that situation for several more months, and my family had ended up on the streets. How would I have been treated by people I came into contact with? How would I have wanted others to treat my family? Who would have wanted to help an able-bodied man with four children and a wife? Although I did not get to that point, it is a real situation for so many on a daily basis.

There are legitimate reasons that a person's life may be turned upside down. Some of these issues are sometimes unavoidable, and they hit people without warning (see below).

The Golden Rule gives me the empathy that is required in my faith to truly understand the challenges of those who are in need. I definitely try to understand why someone is homeless, stranded, or down and out. I also try to make sure I don't have a wall around my heart that would stop me from showing compassion and helping others.

> **Legitimate Reasons Some May End Up Homeless**
>
> Unemployment
> Downturn in the economy
> Rising health-care costs
> Unaffordable housing
> Natural disasters
> Lack of federal, state, and local funding
> Domestic violence

My Purpose as Outlined in the book of James and his explanation of Faith and Works

The book of James in the New Testament reads as follows:

> What good is it, my brother or sister, if someone claims
> to have faith but does not have works? Can this kind
> of faith save him? If a brother or sister is poorly clothed
> and lacks daily food, and one of you say to them, Go
> in peace, keep warm and eat well, but you do not give
> them what the body needs, what good is it? So also
> faith, if it does not have works, is dead being by itself.
> But someone will say, "You have faith and I have works."
> Show me your faith without works and I will show you
> faith by my works. (James 2:14–18)

This is the action of faith that drives the results of my purpose. My faith is shown through my obedience in my works.

When I was at Oakville Missionary Baptist Church in Memphis, Tennessee, Pastor Richmond Savage told me, "Brother Brooks, talk is cheap, but it takes money to buy land." I can correlate what he was saying to the book of James.

We can all talk about what we would do and how much we believe, but do our actions support our words? Whether it is the Good Samaritan or the Golden Rule, how do our actions magnify our beliefs? In my case, my efforts to help the homeless, stranded, and down and out, are connected to my signature program called We Care. This program hands out care packages and information, hygiene kits, and snack packages to the homeless, stranded, and down and out along with the blanket, socks, rain ponchos and knit caps as part of the B&S Program. But it also requires me to explain my purpose and converse with a person to understand how they ended up in their current situations and to lead them to the resources that can help. All packages include the following letter:

> Being homeless, stranded, or down and out are not choices that individuals wake up and make. Today we want to let you know that there is someone who cares. We are trying to do our part through our "We Care" program. The small gift we pass out hopefully can help nourish the body, mind and soul. The Bible tells us that "I can do all things through Christ who strengthens me" (Philippians 4:13). At BBV2M LLC, we practice that and believe it. We are hopeful that our gift brightens the day and gives encouragement to those in need.

The care package is designed to give people a few of life's necessities and steer them to food pantries, shelters, employment agencies, medical facilities, and legal help in the area.

Care Package Content

It is our goal that these few items and the information that is included become "the bridge" that guide people toward assistance. As I think about the scripture and its guidance, I feel it does not benefit an individual if I only offer money without direction. That is not to say that there are not occasions where I may give someone only financial assistance, but I try to limit that as I think about the Chinese proverb:

> Give a man a fish, and you feed him for the day; teach
> a man to fish, and you feed him for a life time.

Types of Care Packages

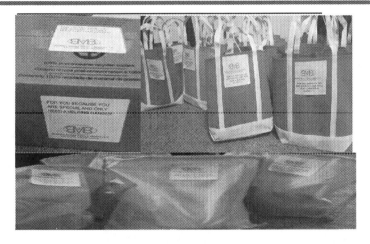

Our actions, driven by James 2:14–18, are not limited to the homeless, stranded, and down and out, but include educating and informing others through our literature. We have created several informational pamphlets and a website to assist us in this endeavor.

Website

The Question: What Have I Really Done to Have an Impact on Others' Lives?

One day while I was listening to Moody/AFR radio, the speaker said there comes a point in everyone's life where he reflects on what he has accomplished or the meaning of life. He said an individual usually starts to ask these questions in his forties and added that as you ponder these questions, you go through a checklist of your accomplishments that relate to family, job, education, awards, and overall wealth. Then the person might look at his social status and compare his accomplishments to those of others or to his original plans for his life. He either will be happy or, most likely, disappointed. The disappointment lingers as he thinks about missed or wasted opportunities. He may even ask himself, what is my legacy or what will people remember about me?

I went through such a process of wondering when I turned fifty. I dissected my family accomplishments from my upbringing to my marriage to the raising of my kids. I looked at my years of work with various Fortune 100 and 500 companies. I analyzed my education over the years and its impact on my life. It seemed that I'd spent my whole life helping others. In the work environment, I measured success by how many of my supervisees were promoted to higher roles. Not that this is a bad thing, but it appeared to me that a lot of the help I had offered had been out of obligation. For me, that meant that the inspiration for my assistance arose from my head rather than my heart.

Jesus asked Peter, "Do you love me?" Peter answered yes. Then Jesus replied, "Feed my sheep." I am not Peter but I did ask myself what I had done for God. My answer was nothing, at least not at the level that I truly believe it should have been. I believe Jesus would ask me the same question: "do you love me? If so, what is the proof that you are feeding my sheep." I return to my scriptural foundation for the answer on why I help the homeless, stranded, and down and out (i.e., God's sheep). There are many causes (sheep) to tend to, and I was directed toward the causes of the homeless in which I felt supported my purpose of helping people out of my heart within scripture and not my head. (the Good Samaritan, the Golden Rule and Faith and Works). Scripture tells us, "The harvest is plentiful, but the laborers are few" (James 9:37).

Throughout my life, I have passed many strangers on the side of the road, but I did not feel true compassion. I have not done unto others as I would have them do to me. I spoke about my faith quite eloquently but yet the manifestation of my works did not bear real fruit. I reached a turning point about what I wanted to do, and the sheep that I seek to feed are the homeless, stranded, and down and out.

How Do I Want to Be Remembered?

Legacy: how a person will be remembered, the contributions they made or didn't make while they were alive.

All of us have the ability to affect our legacies, based upon our efforts and how we affect others. I want to be remembered for how well I followed the scripture while helping those in need and how my efforts had a positive impact on the lives of those who are less fortunate. On Earth, I want to be remembered as one of many who tried to feed the sheep in a manner that showed compassion while truly helping them at the same time.

That is my purpose, and that is who I am. I am just one of the many legs on the millipede, trying to help the body move in the right direction in the fight to help the homeless, stranded, and down and out. My call to you is not about helping the homeless but about finding your purpose and finding a way to achieve it. I do hope, however, that your purpose includes finding ways to help those who are less fortunate.

CHAPTER 12
The Millipede Effect

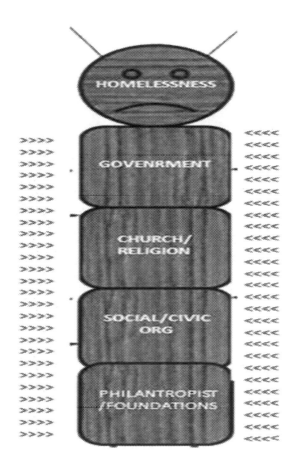

As I described in the first chapter of this book, the body of the millipede is similar to a long train with connecting railcars. But unlike a train, one side of the millipede does have the ability to work move independently from the other side. The millipede's first and last segments each has a single pair of legs while the rest of the body has two sets of legs. As the millipede grows, it adds segments to the body and legs to each segment. The millipede moves very slowly, but it needs all of its legs working together and in sync to do so. Each pair of legs on one side moves together while the opposite side moves together, giving the millipede a rippling effect when it is moving.

What I have discovered in my quest to understand the homeless, stranded, and down and out is that the problem is similar to a millipede. The fight to help the homeless has multiple parts, just as the millipede does, that are separate but interconnected. As I discussed in earlier chapters, government, religious, and charitable organizations are interconnected in their efforts to help the homeless.

Coordination and support is critical to the support of each group. An example is a federal grant program that is offered to state or social and civic organizations. What makes the millipede move are its many legs, just as the countless number of people who work and volunteer at the various organizations are the reasons for their success.

Like the legs of millipede, people don't always move together at the same time. The efforts appear disjointed or slow at times but the ultimate goal is accomplished. Without its legs the millipede cannot move, and without the people the process of helping the homeless does not happen. The movement of the millipede's legs in unison is similar to people having a common cause and working together to achieve it. Below is a comparison of the millipede and the homeless:

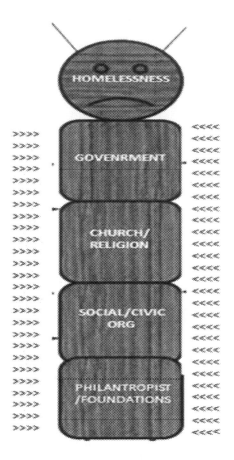

1. It does not have a thousand legs but the number is vast similar to the number of people helping the homeless.

2. It is vulnerable to other predators and parasites, just as those who are homeless are vulnerable to mental or physical challenges or domestic violence.

3. Millipedes are harmless but can be considered nuisances or pests. In some cities, local governments have passed ordinances to remove the homeless from certain areas.

4. Millipedes sometimes are thought to have exploded in numbers. The number of homeless may grow depending on various circumstances.

5. There are various species of millipedes. There are various reasons individuals become homeless, including economic conditions, medical issues, natural disasters, etc.

6. Similar to the nuisance aspect, most people prefer not to have the millipedes around.

Perceptions of the Homeless
- They are criminals.
- They are con artists.
- They are lazy and don't want to work.
- They are drug addicts and winos.
- They are mentally ill.
- They are disabled.

CHAPTER 13

What Have I Learned?

My Quest to Understand and Help the Homeless, Stranded, and Down and Out

A key conclusion that I have come to in my search for knowledge about how to help others is this:

There Is a Problem and the Problem Is Not Going Away.

From large cities to small towns, the problem is the same for those who are homeless, stranded, and down and out. I stopped in Bastrop, Louisiana (population of about 11,000), and ran into a gentleman. I gave him a package and had a great conversation with him. He told me that the mill had closed, there were fewer jobs in town, and it had had an impact on everyone. Crime had risen and that he was just trying to survive. That is a common theme: people are just trying to survive, sometimes by any means necessary. Most of those I have encountered really would like to change their situation. However if you are faced with the same grim circumstances each day, they eventually become a way life, and you cannot think of any alternatives.

When I look at the major institutions that are tackling this problem, I am filled with a sense of pride. Government, religious, and charitable organizations do a tremendous job. One could ask what there is left to do, as these institutions have made it part of their DNA to fight this problem.

The millions of people who serve and volunteer with a passion for tackling this problem are truly unbelievable. People of various ages, races, and genders; from small towns and large cities, are on the front lines of this cause. These volunteers and servants put their money, time, resources and brain power into this never-ending process. I am overwhelmed with pride to see people work tirelessly from soup kitchens to the halls of the legislative branches of government. This is a sacrifice for some—there is no payday for their actions—and others have bypassed more lucrative opportunities. Many individuals live the parable of the Good Samaritan on a daily basis. Some do it through finances; others through their efforts. There is a lady in Jackson, Mississippi, who prepares bagged lunches with hot soup in the winter and feeds the homeless. That is what makes America such a compassionate and caring country. That is purpose.

Homelessness is nondiscriminatory. Age, race, sex, national origin, religion, disability, veteran status, income status, and region of the country do not matter. It affects all parts of our society. I have met and talked with many homeless individuals, and each one has a different story. Some have a ray of hope that things will change, while others see no end in sight. Pride is very strong in the streets, as many have refused any assistance from me. My observation, since I have not been homeless, is that being homeless is mentally tough, and it breaks down the spirit. I still believe that no one wakes up in the morning and makes a choice to be homeless. Some, but not all, have the ability to find a way out. Those who can are constantly looking for ways out while those who cannot become dependent on others and are trapped into a state of despair. I pray that I receive the strength to help those who are in need and to be one of the many soldiers on the battlefield in this fight.

NOTES

1. Hopkin, Stephen P.; Read, Helen J. (1992). The Biology of Millipedes. Oxford: Oxford University Press. ISBN 0198576994.
2. HUD Exchange -https://www.hudexchange.info/homelessness -assistance/hearth-act/
3. Source Data Domestic Violence.Org
4. The Parable of the Good Samaritan – King James Bible

Printed in the United States
By Bookmasters